manic pixie dream queer

the sunlight sessions

sage sunlight

BookLeaf Publishing
India | USA | UK

Made with ❤ on the BookLeaf Publishing Platform
www.bookleafpub.in
www.bookleafpub.com

Dedication

for little g, the queer/trans community, and
my family, blood, and chosen.

Acknowledgments

to my therapist:
thank you for your continued guidance and for allowing me a space to unpack my past traumas.

to dad:
I love you and wish we could have gone on this journey together.

Acknowledgements

Preface

to finding sunlight through clouds of despair.
to life, death, rebirth, and acceptance,
while continuing to choose kindness.

1. When's the last time you showered?

you love my overgrown acrylics
barley hanging on for lifeeee
I need a refill
on my meds, so I don't die!

I mean we all gotta go some way
doesn't seem 222 far off from daddy
just another addict running from problems in our heads.

I wanna do better,
truly wanna make ya proud of me,
I wanna like me...
how could you love me?
when you don't even know
the snowstorms of my past?

mama's only child
I made it since she passed...
my older sister didn't make it home.
so how could I ever take

another child from you.

when's the last time you showered?
not coming for you babe,
just worried about you...
depression runs deep but will forever choose
to be kind.

2. sage solana sunlight, the fairy.

I love being the one that ya fumbled
stumbled down so much wasted time
I wonder what about my wonder
wanderlust companion...
made you rediscover the
sparkles underneath

i've been the same girl, same sis
sage sunlight

the first state manifesto
center stage spotlight
simmering, sizzling summer
soon to be zapped to memories

am I just an addict who uses people
or simply,
is my life just in sunny despair?
"smile nice & big for the..."

destined to be a fairy

embrace the whimsy
little miss 1318 & change.

yeah, alright
maybe I prefer the limited edition
short lived, infamous in a decade
past its prime
runaway bride high on her should've been
wedding night
instead booking flights
for free thanks to daddy
it's the least I deserve
senior walked, now I run
to a destination remaining
unknown, will I ever find
my own, truly a land
I can call
home.

3. lines

sunrise with you
or maybe just
sleeping in till noon

the light of your smile
it's driving me blind
traveling miles
to two different towns

I mean what if?

we can just roll along with the flow
and the bright glow of newfound
love? lush fun,
you're more than just another fuck—

will I see u later?
I won't be the one
to ask if you'll be my baby
i've gone out on so many
lines can't lie to my mama
can't lie to myself

from the lines on scattered papers
never filed for,
would I still try lines
like dad did
if we had just left him
would this childhood trauma
still lead to a love for drama
escapism & reckless fun
like snowflakes
can we swift on by
explore the flurries turned frenzy

you feel the energy too
grab the rush, turn it up
sweat tour live on the apartment floors
sorry to your neighbors!
two sparkling creators
well yeah, we're currently waiters
but this love of labor
needs you to break her
face life in minimal mode
forever that party girl
just hit the floor without the alc
now hand me the aux!

4. it's important to read, stop scrolling

scared of these falling literacy rates,
am I failing them,
by following the guidelines above me
in a new era of ED.
if it's above me and I don't feel like reaching...
then I won't,
not like I get much of a tax quote
but i'll forever make it work sis...

one thing about me
at any age
i'm still gonna fall
for the impossible guy

is it bc i'm scared of rejection?
you can sense it, can't u?
magical malachite
serpentine back home
but they'll meet again

one day soon

no more friend gloom
can't wait to watch
our stars rise & grow.

5. $1,300/week

losing identity
but i'm a prophecy.

let me make my own mistakes
lived through my parents
let me make my own mess
fuck! i've always had to have it together,
give me a break
so what if I do a little coke
every couple of months
my daddy did it my whole life
then had the nerve to fucking die...

before I could talk about it
with him, 365 bumpin that
just once with him
fuck that would've been cunt
but still I know
this ain't my drug of
choice
to be a whore
sex addict
I need to work on it

for gain and my own interests

nothing wrong with dipping your toe in the
oldest game we can name
I make you feel good, you help me
and then we both leave happy

can't tell me that i'm wrong
providing a service
public education says
$1,300 biweekly
thirteen hundred a fucking week...

he says 1000 for 2.5 hours
but it's more like 45 mins if i'm being honest.

stallion take your time!!! listen, you'd do it too. you don't know where I fucking came from, i'm lucky to even be alive, okay?

6. glaceon

always been an ice queen
glaceon forever on me
snow snuck my daddy
I guess charli was right

childhood judging
adulthood researching
maybe i'll find the answer?
generations of black trauma
can't blame you for the addictions
even on my meds and a good day
I still somewhat crave the escape

scared imma log off
and leave my pc on
a journey that would break her
I fear for the day she's gone
and i'm left, right yeah, okay

call me out on my bullshit
make me feel fucking stupid
i'm self destructing before your eyes
yet you turn a blind eye...

not your fault tho,
going through it with a husband
is one thing, but to watch your son
the favorite grandson...
just think of what he could have become.

7. island

am I wrong?
for being a party girl
it's not 365
just weekends babe!

only a quarter of a century
you had your phase
while I phased to adult in 2011.

thought u were better than me
when you just had more connection
over your "good black" peer...
thinking of walking away
wish I could see you again
before we're both silver gray

pictured thanksgiving day with you
now racing to cum for your ego
scared for next valentine's day
but instead i'll prolly just wake up with
another stomachache

counting days
that's all my days now
not much joy
but wish I could enter back
into the woods bc i'm beyond lost

I won't be found here
in a couple years starring
on broadway theater in the round
ready to reclaim my island.

when I disappear to my island
know i'll send your ticket soon
just nemeses to clear my mind
I always want you near too

I don't know what the fuck is up
I wanna lock in and date soon pls
it's giving gemini forever fleeing
the scene that they created
murdering another
dream of me.

8. key & lock

key & lock
looking for my lock
where do I enter now?

flying hazed
"drunk running"
at this performance
the role of "boyfriend"
will be played by:
u won't be disappointed.

better on stage
always loved crowds
much easier to escape
watching another cityscape
while you hit your superior vape.

babe, one more kiss
on your fire escape
wonder if i'm still a touchy subject
that your next could accept,
will you tell them how we wept?

or will it be a secret well kept?

with all respect
i'll miss finding home in your lock
love, your key.

9. are you being served?

reunions rarely reap the
rainbows & butterflies...
running errands alone now.

nothing in the suburbs for me now
never could have given picture perfect
how can you be loyal to one
when you'd rather say fuck it and call royal
ahhh haha.

when you've never found home
more than just another hole
you believe me?
even if not? that's hot...
i'm sure i'll see you round once more!

overloved, over served
at times curved,
but oh so well preserved,
no longer reserved or nerved,
hi love!

are you being served?

10. the lesson.

thank your teacher
so many lessons learned
from the classroom & beyond
while you may go back
thanking them
most times the lessons go
absorbed, activated
long away from the formative time.

being my own profession
you think i'd remember that
but i'll thank you now
the year I spent with you
changed, shifted, molded me
for good.

wish we could have experienced
magical fairy tale lands longer
however forever grateful
for the ride to Oz at all
now it's back to

might be time to stop smoking

green yet funds stay low
11 days free from alc
miss MJ will u be next?

only time will tell
when you live to see an age you never
imagined you learn to just take it
one day at a time.
sometimes you're not fine
believe me, you won't find it
in another dime.

11. horny in your hometown

3 am tears carrying hurt stroll down
my face, heart & soul feel lost
changing for good,
while still longing for the past.

daily battles with depression, anxiety, and
substance abuse
learned from senior, unc & pop-pop

such a heaven burden to hold
that most are unaware I hold daily
meds, weekly therapy, and I could
still say fuck it all and go on a bender

I wish my brain would settle,
growth & progress indeed
but i'm slowly getting tired of this fight
if i'm being completely honest
tired of toying with goodbye.

nothin like being horny in ya hometown.

why do you still feel the need to escape?
daily meds in my bloodstream
but i'm still fighting me
I know what to do, but I don't wanna do it,
time to do it before there's no choice.

emotionally heightened yet scared
biting the hand extended
is it too late for an olive branch?
you've been fighting this battle for years—

you look great!!
thanks I haven't eaten in days and strictly
consume alc & weed!

what!! you know i'd never cross that
lineeee, hmmm maybe just one more
lieeee telling myself I wouldn't
jump zones, but fuck!!

we've been out here so long,
but I still wonder...
will I always still have a little thunder
or will I stumble &

go
under.

12. keynote speaker

you were on survival mode
new game setting unlocked

you were never too heavy
so he couldn't hold you,
or maybe you let go

they always claim to be strong
history shows he can't back it up
easy to fuck but hard to love

almost 10
years in the game,
"is it okay i'm only 15?"
giving you the out,
but you just want me to eat
you out then bounce

one side is complete
while the other just received their
diagnosis
how much longer?

leash held by you
you lead & I go.

just another queer with daddy issues
you may paint me as
but do you want me to expose
the time your dad painted me?
I choose kindness and light
darkness consumes
childhood.

you're still satisfied with this subscription
right?

I love you not so bright
bedroom nightlights
blessed for my brother,
for some reason, i'm still here.
silly, whimsical bachelor...
I choose to teach her
tearing at your future
welcome our keynote speaker.

13. by thirty

flashbacks to the past
now fast forward
to my dad
flashbacks of HIM now.

why do things always
have to go your way?
why do I fall in line
instead of taking a stance?
no tank tops
I always felt sexiest in a tank—
top well
beautiful broadway brown baby
check boxes
a colored of substance

I loved you
& lost me.
stood up for me
& lost you,
ending declared by one...
unfollow mutuals and each other

before we part—
I fell in line; i'm not sure why.

maybe because I still loved you,
more than I loved myself
found value all alone,
thanks for loving parts of me—
my next will love every part of me,
feel blessed for access to me beyond
the marquis, hope you're mine by thirty.

14. do you really love nature?

holding on 444 dear life
leaves & trees, seasons change
the way we do, colors eras changing
but we'll always come back
see you next go around
blossom, bloom, bottom bunk
before the winter breaks us.

winds wandering into business
when she should mind her own
our leaves wavering, wanderlust
landing on unfamiliar grounds—
God ground my soul.

could you fall in love with a tree?
could you last through my winter?
too much full bloom comes in joyous june?
fall into the new possibilities
bend & spring into a comeback.
and if you'd rather cut this oak
you'll miss my magic...

just ask your Dad.

fall into the new possibilities
bend & spring into a comeback.
and if you'd rather cut this oak
you'll miss my magic...
but i don't think
you really love nature.

15. dream of me?

I wanna touch ya
but you're too damn far away!
AHHHHH
come & roll up with me
don't have to be so sweet

little white lines
single bill so tight and right!
it's always better high
even tho that I
know i'm choosing to die.

what can you do when
you don't even wanna fight for you?
what can you do when
you're on the meds but sabotage yourself—
missing days, got no days to take off bc of the
mental breakdown I had earlier this year

whew...
but they don't care about that.

if I died, you'd have to find another body, so
let me take care of my body
my mind's not right; i'm trying, fighting hard
fuck—i'm getting tired of trying what the
fuck am I fighting for

so many I love,
so many that love me!
born in 1999
don't know who i'll reach
but my message runs deep
choose kindness, please just try...
you may not ever know,
just how much that your glow
guided a new angel to their wings.
that's the good word, at least to me,
first state "hippie"
the manic pixie of ur dreams

could be dreaming next to me...
but I still won't save your caller id
can't make you vip
not used to sensuality
but that's me,
now go and explore

it's not me—
just you're manic pixie dream.

16. virgo

scared to ask for help
but always giving a helping hand
prepared to change for lovers
while abandoning him.

you've always been special
had a light about you only others could see
now you see your magic
let's explore it babe!

fought silent wars
while generations praised you
always deliver a stellar show
mommy & daddy so different
here with you all vs. at home.

love them and everyone else now.
felt so alone as a child, young adult
twenty five year old, now...
I hope to be close one day,
racing down the highway
my hand on your thigh
just one more time?

song as catchy as a nursery rhyme
they're screaming showtime
but i'll risk it all for you anytime
everytime fuck it's not a crime
you & I together will always be our prime,
hope you're mine by
wintertime
my sweet piano virgo boy.

17. kindness

maybe it's time
to stop choosing kindness
seeing as they always choose violence &
rhetoric that replaces the blame
back to the black & brown
broken down, barely there
parents.
but that's white
private school kids
"leading" a title one school

marble nails
one green
one pink
wicked magic inspired.
everyday spinning new spells
screaming SOS save my students
youth of america, i'm sorry
one day we'll make things right
not even that I hate you whites,
but I'll never benefit from being light.

18. mom-mom

i'm 25, this is my time
seamstress sensation for decades
doing it for doris ray and doris faye
two iconic women
walked so mom could run
now I can stun!
holding on to their passion!!
new york apartment tour
is where i'll be,
drag queen, writer, english teacher
I can do it all,
jack of all trades
master of none, but i'm down for one!
just be open; you're not just anyone
#1 forever in my eyes!!!

you always said "favorite grandson"
witty & wise, wondering why I couldn't have
had more time!
youngest brewer yet i'm not bitter
if my parents did their best,
fuck self pity, I wake & choose peace

difficult every day, put on a brave face
not saving any race, but I do my best
mental illness—affected this seed long before
our harvesting
sorry i'm late, was gardening
being honest to yourself is the hardest thing—
learned it at 24
the same hours you're given south...
fuck you sammie—right now you're dead to
me.
until you apologize,
mental health studies, yet coming for me, my
mom & my dad...
you'll always love me, right now it's ugly, but
it doesn't have to be.

apologize please,
aunt crystal always gleamed
supported & heard you out.
she loved a bad man, who was the best friend,
a story reparative in this tree...
we've run the same race, i'm tired of the space
I want my cousin back,
we both know how to give a deserved whack
to bullshit, beyond zodiacs

shared family trauma,
make up with my mama
throw on some pajamas
stream rina sawayama
then stream melodrama...

19. keke!

shoutout to my girl keke
raised on true jackson vp!
truly, that girl & voice
of black excellence
it's our era now
that's not the rep we want
but that's the rep I've got
to find a way to expose the frauds
sitting at the top of pop ready bop
the inner boys club circle
you love to patrol "those" pupils...
eyes dilated from the "founding" days.
how can you discover a neighborhood where
we've been owned our homes.
play your games on the clock
but baby, when i really go off...
keep pushing this tree & you might face:
white man vs. bear.
chile I know who i'm taking!

I hit rock bottom a lot,
thought we all did that?

fuck i'm gonna crash out
without a single doubt
mrs. d quit monday,
said "get railed" i'm going on retirement
can't blame her
don't shade her
not too much on my girl, mrs. d
what you know about those math skills
bookie pls—
it's fun & games till you ignore my request,
straight disrespect
sorry that's just district...
we acknowledge the problem
and avoid solutions... I fear all men are
choosing danny phantom going ghost.

trauma trickling out,
a new chapter to be found
but another manic top
high off white rock—
hold on, hold off on that ending
it's just the beginning of endings
you'll face but each change brings you to a
deeper place, just wait...
you'll see it later babe.

20. magic or tragic?!

my mind is magic
clinically manic
when I walked in bear
before I became bare
look at garebear
bipolar depressant
prince of passion passing
pre-sneaking pedos 444
parts pulled
powerfully punted
straight
adulthood
aged around aahh?...
i've never remembered
revered never recovered
bandaids on a kidney infection
somehow still seductive?
I wish I knew who abused me sexually.

but maybe my magical morale
marches with matches
each monday through the door

when i'd decline continued employment if
finances fell to fags like you & i...
fall in love with love one more time
time more one love with love in fall
fell in love, with love one, more time...
"time, wounds love—'with love I fell'."

release it, react to it
researching recent
depressed deeply, anxiously aging to my grave,
all over grades?
how it may perceived to your plan
oh white man...
i'm not the faggot to be fucked with.
you wanted the "nigga" to pop out,
popular, always known about popular...
now pop culture has finally caught up.
visionary, legendary, everyday live before your
eyesssss
on your own paper, not mine, mister!
I wish I could've known you, sister—
sweetly shines me to seeing said;
discrimination enlister

catching you in a silly tongue twister,

all this mess to assist her
wife knows, now you dismiss her?
i'd use a stage whisper
i'm a smart jr glister
could've just been a blister
you don't regret when you kissed her—
not doctor, white Mr.
magic made off of blackness.
moonlight mind made of magic,
my two sides: magic or tragic.

21. satire

passing homegrown
in my hometown
main street delaware
college feels, forever ago
fleeting fantasies—
it's only been 222 years
how could everything change in two,
I know you feel it too.
we're aligned
in touch with my mind
are you listening?
i'm up here glistening
golden goodie garrett-lee
leaving, longing & lusting
lana launching
let's revisit a lust for life
even in dire times,
at least it's just a flat tire
some pray for a flat tire
speeding towards a ball of fire.
the life & times of black queer satire.

22. SR

my dad died a week after my two months of
sobriety at twenty-three.
how to be an almost functional addict:

while wonder & whimsy were wrestling—
nestling, needing norman SR.
it's just a misdemeanor,

reckless driving, alcohol-related.
I studied how to be an almost functional
addict
a little too closely...

august 5th, 2022:
werq the world, bitch!
"have fun & be safe tonight, garrett jr."
daddy's final goodbye—
there's no guidebook to your dad dying while
you're twenty-three,
so close to being free.

on the last set of classes,

a master's in the mirror reaching for me.
never missed a shift,
student placement gig or good sex,
I did it without a smile,
but believe me, my heart was broken.

but little Black boys don't matter—
why can't you just say,
Black lives matter?

taking nothing from you yet,
you play the victim still.
I've always been a queer Black person.
I learned to navigate your world,
but you refuse even to respect mine.
how do you fashion that?

when we're entertainment or status,
you LOVE us... not really—
just wanna own us;
modern-day slavery
in white pockets begging, "please pick me."

play the fame game.
wanna be a name?

get ready for a “hey man,
oh yeah, I came, man.”
you can head out,
a modified American plan.

come early or late,
but boy, not serving
three plates—first state,
fire fighting for his life.

I won’t be owed by a simple
rich white man.
mama, I am a rich man,
a blossoming beautiful
Black queer man.

23. Looking

media lied to me:
"accept it, come out, find him."
the prince has disappeared.

cold and desolate,
pounded by shadows of uncertainty—
I thought it would be different.

burning insecurity,
squirming in disgust.
but I want more than this.

dominantly hesitant,
yet submissively sincere—
I have to do this.

pondering the potent,
glorifying the astonishing,
until the inevitable vanishes.

reflecting in solitude,
lusting for intimacy,

knowing he is gone.

a momentary pleasure—
while still better than none—
has coerced him to become

a cunning casualty,
eternally looking? Looking! Looking...
for fun.

yearning yet remorseful,
still, I pushed on—
eternally looking? Looking! Looking...
for fun.

24. colors

My dad would always say,
Ah, God, I can hear him—
"The only thing I have to do is stay Black and die!"

I'm okay with you calling me
whatever you want,
because at the end of the day,
by day, I don't know—
Should I choose me?
Or you?
Because we both know
only one of us
can truly get what we want here. Ugh.

In the end, we both knew
this was the thundering storm
threatening our tropical,
tenaciously tangible,
triumphantly tragic
true love.

I know we both—
tied together too close,
too soon to launch?
We believed in this—
Please, give it a chance,
full launch, just try for me—
I want you in my life forever,
and I will forever want you
in my life as my—
for him.
(Solo Troye version, please.)

You quite literally
walked me—
wrote the grandiose bestseller,
"How to Save a Life in a Year!"
Only it worked too well—
Depression and anxiety
muddied my many
moments of myself.
My inner voice was silenced;
it was easier to turn my brain off,
to convince it that if I became your M U S E.

Now that I can think clearly,

finally finding finite—
06//03//99—
thank you—
22//'22.

You opened me to a world,
a marvelous life to be lived.
I don't think I could
have ever even slightly imagined...
Finally facing the storm of
"Garrett Lee Norman."

I lay him to rest
as I enter this new era
of exploration, joy,
and most importantly,
L I G H T.
The light was always coming
deep down, maybe,
just maybe, baby,
I knew that.
But I know with all my heart,
you saved me this year.

Craving to experience an open relationship

from a healed place.
F U C K!
You're legit my dream man—
I manifested you into my life.
But I know deep down
I want a partner
that you embody so narrowly yet—
negates Norman's
negligence.

So shit, I'll say—
sunny soft sand,
surfside in hand,
I must now take the stand—

F O U N D G U I L T Y:
in wanting to explore
the deep wonders of before—
a bruised and battered boy
from the Blue Hen state.

Bellowed from deep down below—
Why did I have to heal and realize
there's more to my journey
that needs exploring?

I'd never do it while with you—
not because I don't love you—
you're my espresso...

You made it clear that's not your style,
though—
and it's not what you signed up for.
But knowing there are only two options,
slam the screen door shut
on our story completely
or leave and embrace
the leverage of lasting leaps,
low below.
This was
the love of a
L i f e t i m e.

When I met you, I was red,
you were yellow; yet yesterday,
my yielding, yearning for another
yearlong yellow—
you've become yellow yourself.
Now it's time to find out
just who yellow mellow
Garrett Lee can be.

I pray for the day mellow yellow
Garrett Lee's playfellow era comes.
Can you reinvent red... at least the old him?
O r a n g e s i c l e, o r g a n i s m i c,
o r g a n i z a t i o n
that has always been worthy.

One day down the line, I hope to
form a forest full of
generously green, lush trees,
guiding the inevitable gutting of your trauma
that tirelessly tortured your
T r u t h.

25. miss me

Used to having all eyes on me,
yet here you are, against me—
Why would I care to try harder?
Only love and respect me
when it benefits you.
You've admitted spells of disaster strike
when I'm not here,
yet turn around slyly,
striking me with passive-aggressive
pleasantries.
Do you want me to be here or not?

One foot out the door—
I'm careful about the things I say,
because children do listen.
They won't always show it in real time,
but they are always watching,
looking to us for who to be.
At what point do I listen to myself?
Mental health at an all-time low—
I have nothing left to give you, I'm sorry.
I'm choosing myself for the first time;

I just need you to listen,
not to understand—
You'll finally grasp it
when it impacts your literacy numbers
and you're stuck interviewing
at a Title 1 school
where most kids read
3-4+ grade levels below,
little to no support,
and admins who don't understand your
curriculum.

APPLY NOW!
Apply yourself to putting in the work,
the real work it's going to take
to bring about change.
Oh right—your kids go to private school
and the speciality schools
in our district...
yet you preach about us
soaring above the odds—
Please, Ms. Missy,
miss me with that bullshit.

26. goodbye, garrett.

I'm not the one you marry,
only around to carry
out another cruel, airy-fairy
dream beneath the winter's flowering cherry.

Goodbye, Garrett.
Well... goodbye, Garrett.
It was nice to have you in my life—
honored to know Garrett,
even though Garrett
will never learn to love a partner right.
Wow, wow, wow,
Garrett.
Still playing the fuckboy game—
open or too afraid to open up?

I miss being a unit,
even if I wasn't whole,
longing to call you home
even if we'll never finish building one.

27. mr. norman

enemy #1,
always the "others."
but without us, you wouldn't be here—
you constrict yourself constantly,
yet you know no other way,
straight white man.

I make forty-eight thousand,
six hundred sixty-three dollars a year—
or $1,337 every two weeks.
a second year with a Bachelor in Science—
let that sink in.

trusted to shape the youth,
but paid barely above the poverty line.
thank god for my strong mother—
without her, I wouldn't survive in this career.

you're worried about the little things,
while others are forced to go virtual.
do you want me to be here or not?
I already have one foot out

of the door you're slamming
shut on me and these students.

to my students:
you can do anything you put your heart and
soul into.
mr. norman, forever in your corner—
limited time left in the classroom,
"don't miss his star-turning performance."
the understudies are great,
but you've gotta see Garrett!

choose kindness now and forever—
for me, please.
I will never forget you all.
thank you for everything you've given
this one Black queer.

28. all this over the dolls

escort
nothing wrong with a little
sex work
like she's an expert
in the works
of 45
17-21 to be finite

baby somehow
someway we're always
gonna make it make it
make sense—
tensely holding on to my EX!!!

let's let the wineeee
and the good timessss
hold us byyyyy

don't wanna lieeee

here and dieeee
like all my peers

nothing quite wrong
after all,
we're native
here
miss beautiful
screaming y'alllllll
truly crawlllll
creating brawls
just to end this doll...
all this over the dolls?

29. new friends

missing trains, running trains!
don't wanna be seen or perceived
i'm always feigning for green

friends who fuck
what the fuck
never what we planned
but together we're a treasure
let's unpack that queer trauma
over a patron margarita
could never!
let's jog across
we're truly giving vlog!

summer may be gone
but the support never disappears
summer forever
you should stream "forever"
by my girl miss fletcher
stripped version to be rigid,
I think I could love you forever
& ever & ever & ever

333 on the right,
i'm not turning left,
I promise,
i'll safely land—apollo.
it's more than trains, planes, and thangs,
you're sweet to the core
deserve SO much more,
one day everyone will see that,
but for now at least your new friend
Sees the vision,
fuck I had the best brat summer!

30. ruin

can I see your teddy bear?
for when you're scared &
for when i'm not there,
because anyone disrespecting you
would get an intro to my knuckles!
once you've taught at a title one public
middle school, nothing really scares you...

did I really need this era?
screaming to fletcher
fuck! maybe I am?!
ending another summer solo
that i'd kill to hear sung
just once more, take my hand in yours
I love to explore
the city & more
this energy /// chemistry
I know we both feel it!

please don't ruin this city
you're my ruin—
texas baby

i'd pack & move to italy
maine, fuck maybe even
missouri—
pls let me put you on to chappell!
guess what i'm really saying is
we never have to guess what the vibe is
always so sweet and so ripe
let's start a new apple tree,
it's giving chosen family!

31. gemini vs nyc ivory

one thing y'all ivories gonna have
is nerve baby
let my black ass snap like that—
breaking news: aggressive top!
but that's what you like
the fantasy of it all,
I get the appeal
& i'll happily play the part
pls cast me now!
not the couch—
a tale of one gemini
ebony baby boy's dreams...

even in nyc
still the boy you don't see
or won't see, chose to be
this way is the norm
no blacks/fems,
the list of other than
skinny/white is weaponized
but you chase after our leaks...

bbl, lip implants, botox in your 20's
babe that shit is a little bsc
delusional daydream drifting on by
I enjoyed my travels through one year of the seasons.

32. for them.

I never really drank corona's
much before I knew ya
now it's my midnight
good mourning
to me indeed
starving artist
need to harvest
fuck it's almost halloween
no plans indeed it's true
ready to fully bloom
wanna guess my petals' colors?
hehe just ask nice & i'll show ya!
never bloomed but maybe I will just for you!
for him performed live, that extra verse still...
haunts my mind at 25, the same way she did it
a decade ago!

finishing the night
with corona
dark time capsule
the beginning of the worst
2019

now she was a dream,
I miss watching true jackson vp
come on now keke,
kamala no longer vp

888 years later
and this is STILL the best version of this
song,
god I wish troye would've recorded
a solo version of this song!!!
I swear it just jolts me right back to being a
baby gay
dreaming of meeting guys and having an
actual crush while I was stuck in high school
suburbia hell.
sizzling sunshine,
showcasing stardom starts up.

33. barracuda

barracuda
yeah, a patron margarita!
sipping slow
feeling out the vibe
music bumpin, lights flashing
but too far to really make out
people's faces or intentions
friday night in new york city

good luck babe blasting
now miss cox!!
she killed it in the wiz this summer
truly a living legend you are debora!

nissian navigating nyc friday into saturday—
my night is just
beginning, this is the beginning of the rest of
ya life! just like u said

looking forward to seeing your place,
this is new for us but it's cool
we're on the same page,

we still are right?

I want more memories with you,
I fear I need more memories with you,
I really want you in my life.
near or far from the best,
always looking out for you.

34. jaded pearl

you're jaded
never meant to make you feel barricaded
would've been fun to see les mis but just the
same
assignments still ungraded
at my house though not escaping
confronted with myself
who am i on my own?
not chasing someone to fix me or use as an
escape,
getting tired of tuesday night ego boosts.

new single era,
sizzling & sweet
streaming troye's best
but it thought ten years later
i'd be later along in life—
fuck the judgment.
fuck my judgment of my own judgments
justifying criticism to myself shouldn't be a
question,
working through this, shadow work

hope it works to help me reconnect and come alive.

bumping to good days,
bumping through the night...
fuck i need a good day.
don't tell my therapist,
I pretend that i'm fine,
they all think i'm living the life,
best of both world,
always meant to take over the pearl
what's my dead daddy thinking now?
Fuck it, i can't judge him for his shit,
Then he can't judge me for mine, right?

judgment day comes for all,
I'm fighting the judgments of my judgments.
no need for your echo
Beyonce, no longer Destiny's Child,
all love, just solo, my love.

deeply dreading the decrepit delaware return,
a new york return, no need for concern
closing in on the point of no return,
just like singing to chappell

naked after date one out in soho,
usually all i'm deemed good for.

35. industry hits!

I think my next mistake
just waltzed in,
6 something, fresh cut
in the muscle tank
by yourself?
no plus 111?
let's change that

your looking good on your own
but imagine the throne
we could build
from our brains & beauty
you can have it all
I can have it all
we all can

i'm the abominable snowman
never frosty
no blue balls pls
I carry out the plan
so take your pants off
or let me help ya

three friends,
different yet the same
I miss my trio
pass the mio
order a tequila water
think i'm boutta bus—
back to basics
industry hits!

been in the pits,
still can't do the splits
i'm losing my wits
by the oceanic abysses.

36. shark bowl

on my own tour
exploring the world
different city every night
delly still my hometown
nyc my home now
never home tho
I don't own a house,
trynna create a home
the vision's crystal
clear—get the fuck out of delaware!
babe, i'm trying!!!
just have to land the right part
role, hole, whatever to secure
my place—this space
needs my light
for all the others
I see you,
I hear you
I am you.
we can do anything,
hannah montana
so crazy we started the scalper era...

tickets still bought by bots
but your boy can usually snag a tag
out on insta.
sharing secrets
you've been here since the beginning tho!
I know your face,
thank you for coming back!
also welcome if you're new,
i'm glad you're all here—
we're HERE
in this moment together now.
soon to be a distant memory,
flashback to the past
laughing our asses off
now we're all in different cities.

37. delaware?

destination delaware
down in lower
some say slower
think southern
but suburban &
sunbathing summers
down on rehoboth beach
blues blow bobbie's
the brain may stay, don't sway
newark cops on main street?!
nothing going on in this town
but college kids studying themselves
with some walking out w/ degrees.
what brought you to here?
who actually lives there?
where's the love for delaware?
we lay the blueprint the first print
still mint, diamond & first state.

i'll always have love for you
and all you've done
I couldn't have gotten here

or really anywhere
without delaware
the first state,
without delaware
the diamond state
without delaware
my home base.

a night out at crimson moon
no two nights like any two
1909 W Sixth St.
american bittersweet
sweet treat
american bittersweet
the sweetest treat.

38. Spark!

could've had it all
attended every ball
too bad you slipped
and dipped to your core
hey look the hero lore
could make

how can't you see
i'm not listening
you're still spilling
sippy cup spilled
mom i'm 25
this is getting old
you know I love ya
but I can't host ya
tax-free talk therapy
just logged off with my own
psychiatrist.

my space is invaded
"you're so sensible"
I see this crystal's conscious

and centered crown jewel
spark up as much as my time
you took me to the speak now
world tour august 6th
2011—

aimee & I sipping summertime
a year later I still sing 2011
but from my healed inner kid
we made it past 2011 :)

39. dead dad at twenty-free

I live authentically,
I do it all for me
no matter what you think
but miss tink

that twink—
sleeps alone, but "pls clap
for me," let me clap
your cheeks

only good for fun
i'm always on the run
from really anyone
who wants to be someone

think i'm finally going for,
growing for—
glowing through it all

cinderella you've made it to the ball
welcome to twenty—

f r e e!!!
he's six years
older than me
but he's daddy
to meeeee
miss my daddy
dearlyyyy dear diary

depressed downtown down & out
that was the normie
for garrett-lee growing up in
povertyyyy

daddy does dope
most nights just
to quiet all of the
tightrope
trickling down my sideeee

40. lynch vs ebony

"has anyone ever told you that you look
like—?"

I don't know where to go
what to know
where to go
can I grow?

am I growing old
for this life and these games
I don't know, I don't know
but I should know...

FUCK—
I KNOW I should know—
at twenty fouuuurrrrr
oh wait no more
one higher floor
brain synapses no more than one day
before...

I don't want to be me anymore

guess that's why hindsight's a war
I still feel like a sophomore
kmart superstore department
deplored, uncared for
prisoner of war
ivory vs. the world.

has anyone ever told you that—
your look came from different worlds and
cultures unknown to you by personal choice

my lynch let loose, but damage occurred,
demanded "on the floor"
enter the door, no bed frame, mattress on the
floor, begging for more
magical times on all fours
thanks west chester
for the time to explore
but the door's deadbolt closed.

[double play on my first ex-boyfriend's last name and the history of lynching in the black community.]

41. at least you still have david...

father.
dad.
daddy.
whatever you call em
he's given you trauma.

dads seem to never grow up
major peter pan syndrome
even once they have kids, they fly higher
cuz getting high was the highlight of your life
no one really knew you, but we know who
they are at the core you're so much more than
my coke addicted senior.

I'll miss you forever wonder
what would have become
if mental health was pushed more
so deeply depressed or PTSD past
you served in the marines
lost mommy & daddy at a young age
it's obviously TRAUMA

you have a job to report...
student behavior and reach out to mother
oh she's gone—his sister was there tho
and father still at home
how you'd not see?
he suffered from trauma
though broadcast as trauma
through cokes and whores
he hurt his one true love,
realized his deep love
days before dawn
he's higher in heaven
no more mellow devil
holding him down
he dealt with addiction
but truly twisted with more
mental health matters
black kings losing battles
they could prittle-prattle
around the chore
to tune and service a little brown boy.

42. the lp of us

I wish I could and let go
of this globe and grow
I need him though
it's always been the lp of us.
the best lp I mean he's got some
degrees to deepen the sound
of the best long play sincerely
i'll never spin again
just one more go round
no wait we've fallen down
back in insanity
mental illness diagnosis
you healed way before me
I wonder what would be
if our healed versions met first
you'll always be fond to me
I hope I flash by in your dreams
just briefly, now only a figure
I squint to envision in my mind
you really were major
music & so clever
the virgo way

i'll always have love for u
and you know too
we're magnets together
which sends a sharp sliver
to our hearts
the record won't play now
God how I miss it "wow"
the palace restored
were just renovating
we'll open down the line
of lovers & losses that show up at random
you don't wanna go back
some reason or another
we come back together
it's about time
no this time it's different
we've said that shit billions
of times before
i'll blurt that I love you
whenever I see you
I know that i'll play it again
games over on my end
one life left—
will you connect?
we're better together

i'd like to remember
the spark we share
just one long play jordan
please park in home depot
i'd always carry your flowers
and your fears for falling for me
no longer needed.
I tried for a year and fuck it's so clear
i've never moved
still racing to west chester
university the palpable purple,
golden ram rails
its horns thrown
the lp of us.

43. lemon & lime

you were lemon
I was an open lime
cut the line
lime meets knife
welcome to real life
of miss espolon white
oh fuck yeah, she'll get you right
but you know she cost a priceee haha
make sure to bring big bright green limeeeee
pls don't decline
otherwise we can't go on this ride
oh fun high in the glimmering sky
fantasies fulfilled before my time
expires—this lime lands home early!
you were lemon, but i'm always lime
i'll always long for a good timeeee
which meant our days were
click click tiktok scrolling away
but to this day i'll always be thankful,
love like!

44. did i get the role?!

autumn leaves,
auntie dreams
drifting delicately
down till dawn
dawning, it's your first
fall.
beauty & bliss
blowing bushes
branches & barking

we take for granted
the beauty of nature
blessed creation

zooming the backyard.
zoomed for my bachelor's...
new age educator, also
educated in the same yet different.
my colleagues were my schoolteachers, i've
lived through the shift of education in this
country, and i'm genuinely scared for the lack
of literacy & motivation in our youth... but if

they put their name on the assignment per
your contract, you must give them a 50%

yet once they're pushed to graduation,
a line carefully constructed to remain
remarkable— remarkably red iready scores.

you may pretend to care about kids,
convinced you're cultured & saving the poor
children of color.
it's clear you don't value people,
color will always matter,
where are you trending?

first marking period profoundly pessimistic,
proud of your boy
no longer your toy
token black queer that falls in line
ensemble, understudy this role,
standby for a time, congrats on your first
principal
year two in show,
cancel context "rainbow."
the best shows don't always receive the
lengthy runs deserved,

but there's always a chance of a revival when
the world wakes up, one day they'll be ready.

45. gritty

these streets are mean & gritty
chris sit down stop hitting the gritty
grains of sand sticks sensually
will always waltz on bye
so please don't cry
wash the bullshit auto tears
you're looking quite disturbed—
lovestruck in the city
our celestial city
goddamn what a pity
location: boroughs of
new york city.

46. can we

why do I still miss you?
it's been 9 months...
still forever on my mind
i'm sorry for february
I knew it wasn't you there
but part of me still needed to know
i'm sorry I didn't call
i've never been suitable for my word
I know you're so much better off
it doesn't matter how many times the radio blares
"one last time"
scared you're my "eternal sunshine"
we'll never learn
it's time to move on
can we finally do it?
instead of hurting others
using them as distractions
do you want me or not?
i'm willing to be the partner you deserve.
can we do it for real this time?
I think we can. I believe we can...

can we?
can we?
he took me to the garage I used to park at to
see you, jord.
asked if it was triggering and I lied
"no not all don't worry"
he should have been worried
Mercato
Those West Chester streets
seeing your old apartment
39 West Market St
I want to go back
can we do it for real this time?
I think we can, I believe we can...
can we?
we can...
i'll love you forever
it's not fair to you or him tho
it's time to leave that forest
end my selfish rat race
even tho you'll always play the keys to my
heart
my piano king...
we can't
we can't

but part of me holds on forever
ik that it isn't fair
to you or him
but i'll always wonder
can we...
can we?
but what if we can?
we can't.

47. juan/victor

never been to seattle
or any west coast
but i'll scream lana
till i'm lying under
joy!
woods,
into the woods,
last show—
I can't believe we lost Gavin.

support that artist
thirteen with headshots
little garrett dreamed
living vicariously
through dreams
(to him, delusions)
you've always been right
ahead, they'll get into it
ten years from now.

colombia born
& bread—

show first of course
she's a lady
known for her crazy
should prolly get on prep
certainly not prep during plan
that's yap, then dissociate block.

the dickens to start
maybe industry bar next?
thank u, broadway
broadway thanks u
go see a show
implore the weird
I KNOW you watched glee girl
nothing's confusing
you like musicals,
you just don't know that yet!

48. suburban queers

Tank top
Tops off
The clock's ticking too fast
No masking, no masc kings
Unless they're playing a part
I know I do
Give manly too
Intentionally with jewelry
To balance it out
But that's me, not the whole tree
My branches bestowed me
Like night and day, deeply
Two closeted queens
While I march behind
He's DL and handsome
I always wanted some—
But I was his friend
He trusted me deeply
I treated it cheaply
Scrolling discreetly
With your road
I'm sorry for grindr

You're always a reminder
Of my sins
The evil within
My identical twin
I saw you at the wedding
I know that you saw me
Beyond awkward
I wish I could tell ya
I value your friendship
Once it left...
I'll always be sorry
And now you despise me
As you rightfully sow
The tear in your tank top
Transports me right back
To running daily
Cross-country and APs
Always around me
My secret queer friend
I let lust linger
Leaking the substantial middle finger
Who outs a freethinker
A fellow community leader
Whose road differs
Same direction—two routes

I’m sorry for outing you,
It always turns me blue
To even think how much I hurt you...
You were such a good friend, and
I fucking trashed it
To the core,
I hope you’re well
Z,
& sipping a daiquiri
You deserve it and more
It’s almost ten years later
I'm only left to wonder
What became
Of the boy, I crushed deeply
But he never did it to me
When he had every right
I’m sorry for catfishing you
One cloudy afternoon
I pray you’re flying royal blue.
Royally blue, to be blunt
I think I loved you.

49. twenty-five!?

Is it truly a crime to still want that at 25?

or if it is a multipart series (book, tv, film)—
"Is it truly a crime to still want that
(one)
@20Fine
Or option
(two)
Twenty-Fine!"

"It makes more sense
to
just go along the
guaranteed
Path—" No! My
Darling,
Dazzling,
Declare it official
You're now apart of
this
D Y N A S T Y !!!!!! !!!
!!!!!!!!!

You must always
remember to follow
what you see
vividly, see
washing into your
sparkling potential we
call
L IFE

Wake Up! You're in your
20's with no real adulting
bills, a rent-free home,
and a car that's paid
off—you've certainly done
far more for far less...
Have you ever lost when
it comes to enduring
difficult transitions.

You've done it for as long
as you can remember... nop—
no actually,
I have so much of
my childhood blocked out

that I did seek therapy
and Zoloft to begin my
Healing journey.

Only a
Few months in
but I
Feel that
scorching
sizzle
Of limitless
budding
sunshine
On a perfect
night in
summer,
Shocked still
in
Sensual sparkle
Only— god of
sunlight,
Apollo! To
land on 614
(or perhaps 10
mopar drive)

Simply
Sensational
Side by side
sharing secrets
and sneaky
little peaks
Only to occur
in room 614,
56 s old
baltimore pike

psych meds i'll
forever be
grateful 444

Signing off to
s u m m e r
Because it truly changed
Me—I have been
Changed for good!
Sincerely yours,

garrett lee

Monday, August 19th @
4:08 am... 444
hour till the First
Day of School... (haha)
Yay?!

50. stemming artist

growing up in the time
of the nuclear uprise
on arts
S T E M
you need me!
science: stupid! you've gotta be...
technology's hold reminded me,
why we have lovers & robbers
rolling right through tumblr
Engineering
pc's job—all my life,
the smartest senior software engineer in the
first state
m a t h e m a t i c s
never a subject I mastered,
but baby come soon, i'll be a master in
reading—no, like actually, md. in literacy!
so gay & so right!
baby if u like stem, go for it,
but pls make don't forget about
s t e A m,
arts education or me . . .

51. silly sunset sunshine

beyond thought, just the first idea flowing and writing ideas era haha!

or /// aka (social security system), my debut single!!!! ahhh, so crazy to finally say this has been 20+ years in the making. truly, every connection i've had from birth shaped me; I was born with a brain that needs help to just start where everyone else naturally begins. this is the birth of garrett-lee normie, and i'm so excited to be painting this puzzling picture
purple & proud
family—they all have their quirks,
traumas, drunks & mentally ill, we just don't always talk truth
tall tales turn tan
silly sunset sunshine,
summer swept
stepped, crest & wrecked
& left the quest
wanting to be my own rent

at least at first rent
men
ugh the fantasy rent,
that man for as long as you want him to be
your guest,
please don't leave your crest
you're a gent but—
I leapt, because
unfortunately I need to head west
garrett-lee normie,

the non-binary,
he / they / queer
austin from austin,
oh sweet sunshine
the lone star state,
left his bluebonnet
it's left
kamala
waltzing wishfully wondering
will you wonder what I do?
guess i'll never know decide who,
no, i'm catching my flight to
can't wear white to delight you,
this isn't 1752...

wife who? not beside you—
give pride to
whoever you want beside you!
girl it's been time due !!!

52. my memories made in media

pls steal my summer sweetie
sweaty summer standing forever
still in my mind

so starry eyed
I know you're a
star—shining,
sizzling sunshine
steals my summer,
summer comes again
starting saturday,
stepping into the show
at this performance, the role
of star will be played by you.

53. gay white man

—poem/song idea basically just showcasing how, no matter our love, you could never fully understand my background—

craving converse
crazy converse
coming 20—
2020
covid clouds
cancelled crowds
crowd control
crown ctrl
she's royal, no?
summer, soloana
sunshine supermodel
she screamed
SOS
still stuck standing
still stuck banding
to shit we know doesn't work
choose you
your hope—

for things that fill your soul
so what, if the public thinks it's just
so-so?
speaks to souls who
sweetly receive it,
just like teaching
you're under appreciated

white man,
somehow still always attracted
to you, preprogrammed—
performative part
assigned 222 but,
is that really what,
you, garrett-lee
really wants?
but when we meet!
convos with no clothes
feeling inspired all summer long

I am my own rich man
& stunning woman
healthy human headed
to miss mills,
still serving meals and milestones

mere moments of magic made me
come carelessly
home.

54. delaware diary days

Dear,

delaware diaries,
destroyed days of
dysfunction
drowning deep, deep
down the rabbit hole of
black dysfunction
how could I ever fucking be—
heaven knows
always been a bad girl
sad man, mad them!!!
sending my S O S,
I was always special
we've always been special
the world's just finally
catching the FUCK on
we are the culture
we are the creators
first state saints, but always
democratically devious

tax-free queen!
just a queer suburban teen,
now & always baby

55. I can see the branches on the trees!

wow, I never realized
just how much you'd change
my life lived with love lost

new student asking why I cut my hair
boy, what I thought no one even cared
i've been low, long live lethargic
zoloft zoey nyc 2017

I wonder how medicated garrett-lee
would have done at hofstra
was always so depressed and anxious
my own worst enemy,
but also best friend...

through my headache hurricane hurt
sick mind telling me you could never
I accepted the never
but I resign

mentally at least

new york city
poetry, lyricism, lusting for life
once more, come on norman
you're a fucking norman ROCK
wall is down, no more clouds

I can finally see the branches on the tree,
life begins...

56. Sister

can I get that bartender?
tend to me baby
wherever you're from
i'm following you there
we're eying midnight
by morning a fleeting memory
but you left ur fleet...
never anything worth coming back
444
that's the role of this sweet whore
seduction second nature
gemini babe
this is primal.

clean that bar area
idk what's shining more
can't describe the vibe
not giving miss moon
maybe a girl cute, half relative
to call you my "sibling"

I don't count any of my half siblings

as my family
i'm crystal's only child:
my sister passed,
tossing torches in
june of '99

I am her.
he / they and more,
you're always with me
channel the fem & masc
norman & brewer
now i'm a normie,
garrett-lee normie.

57. october first

I miss exit 7
meeting my ex
plymouth meeting miss taking that exit
476 such a quick little bit
of a ride racing to the revival
you helped revive me
rescued and survived me
glad you made it out whole
forever wanting more
even tho you've got the golden hole
you were everything,
ik that you're better,
no one stuck with bitter
berries broken run down
one year in fantasyland
real for the occupants
I wonder how you respond
questions about me,
what happened, no really?
you two were perfect
grew to different cities
I know you think of me,

the star reversed
maisie is the good witch
conan the suburban king
ready to rule to throne
my life finally in control
well, more than before,
soon to be,
future philadelphia queen
a music whore
culture runs so damn deep,
sports, concerts, or anything
philly goes hard,
theater of the obsessed
foundry & the fillmore,
tla, mann center,
union transfer—
fuck we're at the wells fargo
center of me!
the best of both worlds tour
december seventeenth
2007 wachovia, back then
you started it all
Citizens bank park and the line
i'll give you my everything
my music home!

yeah, i'm from delaware,
hometown show even tho
let's lose our minds,
escape here with me,
never to repeat,
this is one of a kind
I hope you're ready
you're in for a fucking treat
not short, but i'm sweet
another high gemini
haunted family tree,
changing history—
like lin marie
I wanna share my community
it's our time
& maisie's right,
you're just a boy
& i'm kind of the (wo)man!

58. Home

come on, fly on high with me,
never to fly on to a home with he.

code names
with your parents
team gemini
vs. two male robins
I see, see
the game in target
been a month since i've seen you last
may never see you again,
which is the scariest part
but i'll always respect your wishes
and manifest both of our growth
just from afar
I wonder if cece will be on your next team. I
mean muna named
stayaway for you girl
never have been good at being gone
like a friendly ghost grounded in grief
they're just now processing 25 years
too late, maybe next go around.

time to sip that depressant
lay low, landslide live
I mean, of course, you would cry.
lie in bed rereading 13 reasons why
i'm like 99.9%
i'll never be satisfied...

just one more pizza pie from tony-a's
all I need, but ik you need to never hear from
me again,

I hope one day to visit your home,
I may never have one of my own.

59. sweet sweat sex

sweet sweat sex
everybody LOVES
raymond in cayman
but why does everybody
love to give the HATE and
teach 'em to make a shank
Chris? Section—
is that way!
of course we're friends
that fuck in the city
but I just wanna live single
in a new city
yeah ik the sex is pretty
but it's different hitting
and spinning to bottom
number, god, who's to count?!
I love sex in the city,
can I hit it
i'd still get it
never near me
"battle of philippi"
maybe see you in philly,

a million fawn lilies
can we end the battle & get back
222 the dance floor—or
stay in blasting,
blubbering,
bubbling under me—
idontwannabeyouanymore
so let's fucking explore
nothing wrong with being a whore
love that sweet sweaty sex bumping you
charlotte & mellet:
this party's for you—
hear me out, your ep & channel
saved me,
taking my happy little pill
too early to touch the fun of
gasoline garrett-lee
normie, that's normal to me.
break the rules, sweaty!

60. sauvignon blanc

for the lover who saved me.
sipping sauvignon blanc
out of the noir broadway
staple birthday mug
one at my house,
one at yours...
is it still
"garrett's"
I wonder, whimsically
wonderfully wanting the answer to
be a reminder to reminisce
on the renaissance era
so in love with you
& philly forever

61. Seasons

could we have gotten through another
season, let's see one more season pls

end of summer sweaty backseat
screaming teenage dream
fuck it's fall! finally time to finalize
the blooming pansies on that october
wonderstruck in longwood gardens.

wondering wandering weekends
just you and me and that little voice I
SILENCE! if I don't think about it
another weekend will come & help me
blossom—always been the main winx
but i'm more a flora forgotten foliage fairy
supreme.

eating grapes at midnight, but before the final
grape I ate and ached, acknowledging what
would become undone somewhere in this
inventible
ending.

professor always gives 333 options,
so who will you choose?
mainstream media model,
underground upcoming unknown,
or the uniquely talented... you.

our second summer together
sadly won't be another.

62. Little

so many fucked up things
that one little boy had to see
just for her to realize that the damage,
it is quite deep.

mommy did the best she could with what she
had, and HE!
able to escape with coke
and distant memories

I love you, but
I hate, and I'm not quite over that hate yet
I'd never disagree that
I couldn't do better
but maybe one day we'll see
this apple passed through wars
& germany runs generations deep.

forgive, but don't forget
the struggles of your tree,
they laid out the framework
for you to now pick up—

show them black excellence
superiority,
didn't even ask for it
just fell into our laps...
was never about you
just one single chance to me

all over little egos,
white boys, when will you know?
you hold the power to empower
those who go unseen,
remember queer/black & lgbt+, and please
your wife would hate to find out,
let alone your little niece...
their favorite educator
kept locked so super sealed,
never forget i hold keys
that would certainly correct you.

all because in our skin,
it's better to kill
him then bend—
and snap to musicals and question
our norms, formally norman
but losing it day by day...

still reaching for the sunlight
kinder to myself for sure.

thank you for never
second guessing my beloved,
you fought so hard for me
the least I could've done.

sober era pending,
time to
refine and define
my center,
may not be in that core
but powering through to show up
always.

little garrett
braved the weather
with minimal skill,
i owe it to him
showing him he always was ahead
a fairy that loves dairy
mom-mom gave me ginger ale
i got sick all before six
all for the starring role,

handholding with my homies
hoping we see 30
bright & clearly.

63. blinker

deadlines flying by,
coughing over another blinker
listen i'm not "in waiting" for
my circuit party romeo

ten weeks of freedom
enough time for reinvention
perhaps give in to temptation
where everything is beautiful

further north is calling
time to take the phone off silent
do I take the leap in silence
or remain afraid of failing
from the comfort of my home?

64. strawberry milk

I remember you,
I gave you the wrong card
always a sweet & flirty vibe
where your card never declines
monster ball on the tv
cuties behind the bar
truly what more could you ask for?

birthday crowd rapping nicki
how will the dickens handle it?
where do I stand?
supportive yet silent,
so truly what does that say?

choosing strawberry milk
not white or chocolate
never stood out to me till now
guess I was fruity
even before I knew it
just cosmic, almost as
memorizing as a happy hour
espresso martini

somehow always transform
back into that earlier version
time to forgive and let go
grief too heavy to carry any further
so thank you strawberry milk,
now taking strawberry's power...
all the way to my core.

65. Barron

barron,
bubbling bliss beautifully bent
out of shape

how many chances do I have left?
you can only repeat
the same miserable mess
so many times, share
that you can't afford this
too close to the downfall

sobriety...

get me off the battlefield
may choose to turn the weapon inward
the same way this country
pre decides gen z would be left
to renter

empty bottles, empty bottles
all I seem to stumble on
more torn up than before

there's always gonna be one more song

I don't care how it looks
but I know how it feels
to hear he's here
bet ya wish u could taste & touch
but get it off your mind.

why's it so hard to show up for yourself,
when you'd show up for him, her, or them?
how many lives do I have left?
still choosing escapism,
over showing up for yourself.

new york islander
now that's what I call service

excuse me, 1022?
do you need service today?

when you finally stop
to unpack your family's bags,
you begin to realize

the family across the hall
is but you,
in a different font
picked, protected, preferred?
awake and accept the superior font
presented to YOU
through modern media memories
but as we move the needle
a new york islander
on the rise rapidly roaring
now soaring on my own accord
never to be explained or pretended
take my earth, i'll always have my air.

66. Texas

where's your inspiration come from?
survival skills passed
all the way back where half
of the lineage began
segregated yet superior.

ohio
dreaded long car rides,
all fuzzy and so far now
from the memories I can still see.
so deep in the trauma;
you'll never turn on mama,
but thread the needle
and try again.

family out in texas,
5th grader headed with some music
classic gaga helped me survive
the fame still burns deep inside
time to show it all
unveil the being inside.

67. let's level love

living on level 2,
level 1, the good stuff we need
is not there.

level 2 is there, but it's not consistent
what is constant?
let's talk about it!
we're gonna talk first.

level 3, it's there, but it's faceted or facilitated,
gemstone gripping gripe
prompted by the teacher.

it's almost initiated by the student!
september, october, november
our babies that can do will do,
I have examples.

level 1 expectations not taught to students
because a level 2 says "clearly
communicated—not shown"
we need to realize where we are

through conversation and connection
we can become one.

your objectives have to be posted
what is the why?
and if i'm not sure,
where do i look?

i wasn't paying attention when you were
teaching last school year,
yet this year, yearning yasmine...
receiving the gifts upon us.

68. six weeks

never dial back
lock the fuck in
summer 2025
prince charming isn't coming
cinderella & him mixed in one
no need to hurry

chasing round a bee
why'd they come in 333
while the two are away
the third behind to entertain till
nine or go for, 999

does it truly matter?
of factual reports
to the facility at least,
but boys will be boys and
be cowards together
never to face the floor
until they've run out their last door
no more the truest sinner.

bottle cap snuck below
can't lie, I really wish u would have risen
above all the snow midwest boy,
the snow owned and slowed the man, all now
too late.

nobody failed me babes
always flawed from the sprout
will I ever be done growing?
vines voting 444 party venomous vengeance
greener & grateful for my independence

42. would forever meet with you,
headed up to my room...
never needed costumes
always fit well in the master bedroom.

never was good at baseball
singing for myself in the outfield
but grateful for early access
childhood sleepover confirmed
the core of this whore,
guess it's well time for the underscore.

69. fin

music making,
eardrums blazing
with sizzling sounds
it's been some time,
calling back to simpler times,
hearing nursery rhymes,
how swiftly we sweep from playtime to
showtime
expecting always to deliver the sublime.

last time i fell in love,
springtime brings the prime
before summer stuns and sizzles
sunblock smearing sweaty stains
breaking the chains

could we ever work it out?
sadly, no remix pending
just picking my pen tonight;
inhale, scribble, choking a little
masterpiece almost complete.

is anything ever truly done?
even in death, the living remember.
forever daddy's prize
clone of him
you could call it a revival
cycles circle closer,
clouds conspiring, causing clouding
consciousness,
cannot compete,
comrade.

facing death will allow 444 rebirth...
allows you to choose fuller's earth
choosing kindness towards me,
rewarded & reclaimed my self-worth...

fin.

Printed by Libri Plureos GmbH in Hamburg, Germany

9 789369 532155